PASSPORT TO

AUSTRALIA

Susan Pepper

Franklin Watts

London/New York/Sydney/Toronto

Copyright © 1987 Franklin Watts Limited

First published in Great Britain by
Franklin Watts Limited
12a Golden Square
London W1R 4BA

First published in the USA by
Franklin Watts Inc.
387 Park Avenue South
New York
N.Y. 10016

First published in Australia by
Franklin Watts Australia
14 Mars Road
Lane Cove
NSW 2066

UK ISBN: 0 86313 439 4
US ISBN: 0-531-10270 X
Library of Congress Catalog Card No: 86-50570

Editor: Derek Hall
Design: Edward Kinsey
Illustrations: Hayward Art Group
Consultant: Keith Lye

Photographs: Susan Pepper, Jenny Pepper,
Wally Povy, Chris Fairclough Australian News
and Information Service, Camera Press,
Colorific, Colorsport, BBC Hulton Picture
Library, Leo Mason, South Australia Film
Corporation, Tate Gallery, Victorian Tourism
Commission

Front cover: Chris Fairclough
Back cover: Chris Fairclough

Phototypeset by Keyspools Limited
Color reproduction by Hongkong Graphic Arts
Printed in Belgium

Contents

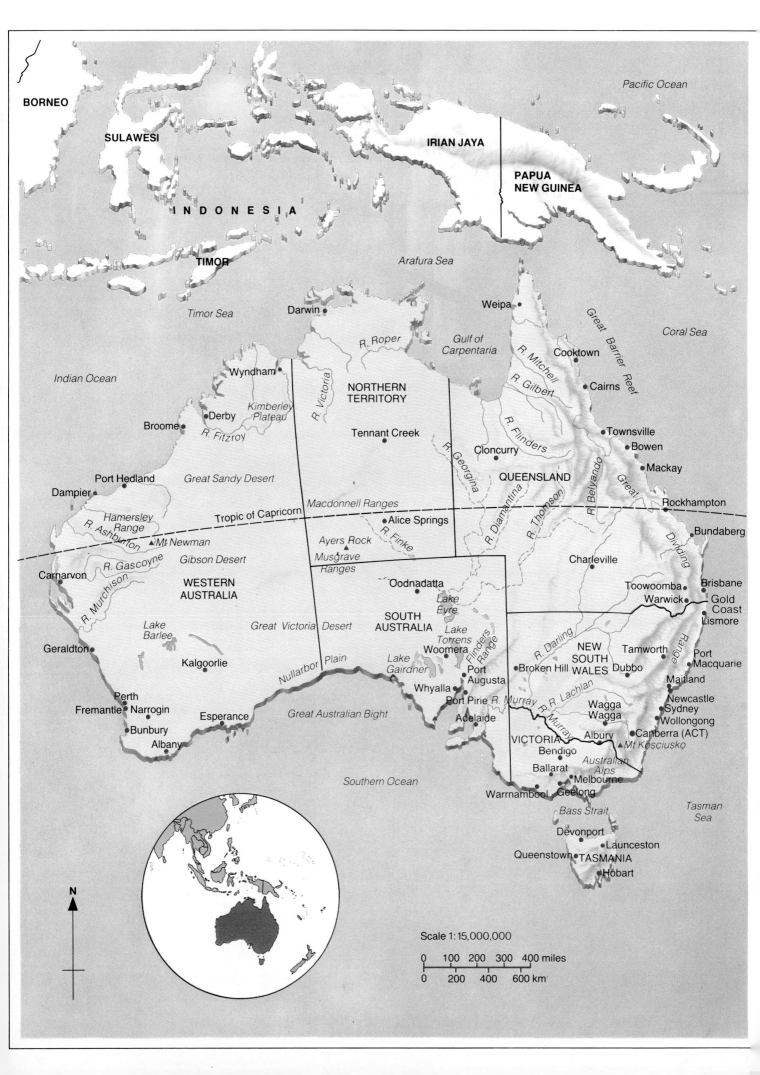

BORNEO

SULAWESI

INDONESIA

TIMOR

IRIAN JAYA

PAPUA
NEW GUINEA

Pacific Ocean

Timor Sea

Arafura Sea

Coral Sea

Indian Ocean

Darwin

Weipa

*Gulf of
Carpentaria*

Great Barrier Reef

Wyndham

R. Roper

R. Victoria

NORTHERN
TERRITORY

R. Mitchell

Cooktown

R. Gilbert

Cairns

Derby

*Kimberley
Plateau*

Townsville
Bowen

Broome

R. Fitzroy

Tennant Creek

R. Flinders

Cloncurry

R. Georgina

QUEENSLAND

Mackay

Port Hedland

Great Sandy Desert

R. Belyando

Great

Dampier

*Hamersley
Range*

R. Ashburton

Macdonnell Ranges

Tropic of Capricorn

Alice Springs

▲ Mt Newman

Ayers Rock

R. Finke

R. Diamantina

R. Thomson

Rockhampton

Bundaberg

Gibson Desert

Musgrave
Ranges ▲

Charleville

Dividing

R. Gascoyne

Carnarvon

WESTERN
AUSTRALIA

R. Murchison

Great Victoria Desert

Oodnadatta

*Lake
Eyre*

SOUTH
AUSTRALIA

*Lake
Torrens*

Flinders Range

Toowoomba

Warwick

Brisbane

Gold
Coast
Lismore

*Lake
Barlee*

Geraldton

Kalgoorlie

Nullarbor Plain

*Lake
Gairdner*

Woomera

Port
Augusta

R. Darling

NEW
SOUTH
WALES

Tamworth

Dubbo

Range

Port
Macquarie

Maitland

Perth
Fremantle
Narrogin
Bunbury
Albany

Esperance

Great Australian Bight

Whyalla

Port Pirie

R. Murray

R. Lachlan

Broken Hill

Adelaide

Wagga
Wagga

Albury

Newcastle
Sydney
Wollongong

Canberra (ACT)

▲ Mt Kosciusko

Southern Ocean

VICTORIA

Bendigo

Ballarat

*Australian
Alps*

Warrnambool

Melbourne
Geelong

Bass Strait

*Tasman
Sea*

Devonport

Launceston

Queenstown

TASMANIA

Hobart

N

Scale 1: 15,000,000

0 100 200 300 400 miles

0   200   400   600 km

Introduction

Australia is a large yet sparsely populated country situated in the Southern Hemisphere. *Australia* means "Unknown Southern Land.". It is a federation of six states, one of which is the island of Tasmania, and two federally administered territories. Australia, together with New Zealand, Papua New Guinea and the islands of the central and south Pacific, comprises the region known as Oceania.

Australia is an influential country within the Southeast Asia region, but also maintains strong links with the British Commonwealth, the United Nations and the United States.

The country is one of dramatic and contrasting scenery. It is also famous for its many unique animals and plants, the probable result of its long isolation from the rest of the world.

Australia's population today is a mixture of the original Aboriginal culture – one of the most ancient and distinctive in the world – and the more recent settlers from Europe and other parts of the world.

Above: The Aboriginal people have an ancient culture. Today only a few still cling to their traditional way of life.

Below: Perth, in Western Australia, provides an excellent example of a modern bustling Australian city.

The land

Australia is an island bordered on the western shoreline by the Indian Ocean, on the east coast by the Pacific Ocean and to the south by the Southern, or Indian, Ocean. The Australian coastline encloses an area almost the size of the United States and more than half as big again as western Europe. It is the world's sixth largest country, but the smallest continent.

Stretching for 2,000 km (1,240 miles) off the northeastern coastline is the Great Barrier Reef, a vast complex of islands and coral reefs.

The flat and semi-arid Great Western Plateau covers much of Western Australia, South Australia, Northern Territory and a part of western Queensland. A famous landmark on the plateau is Ayer's Rock which is a single stone with a circumference of 8 km (5 miles). Australia is the lowest of all continents. Its average height above sea level is only 300 m (1,000 ft), while the average for the rest of the world is 700 m (2,300 ft). Unlike all other continents, Australia has no permanent snowfields.

Above: Some of the animals unique to Australia include the koala, which has become one of the symbols of the country; the kookaburra, a very large kingfisher, which is renowned for its noisy call; the kangaroo, another Australian symbol; and the platypus, a mammal which lays eggs.

Left: Good beaches and rolling surf are found throughout Australia's 19,200 km (12,000 miles) of coastline. Seen here is a tropical coast in the Northern Territory.

The central-eastern lowlands extend from the Gulf of Carpentaria in the north to eastern South Australia. The most extensive uplands, the Great Dividing Range, run along the eastern edge of the continent from Queensland to Tasmania. The highest peak is Mount Kosciusko, in the Snowy Mountains of New South Wales. About a third of Australia is desert.

Almost 40 per cent of Australia is in the tropics and is warm throughout the year. The south has more temperate climates, though winters can be cold and frosty. Australia has, however, less extremes of temperature than other regions of comparable size.

Most of Australia's weather is characterized by clear skies and low rainfall. For this reason the supply of adequate amounts of fresh water is a continual problem, particularly in central Australia where droughts are common. By contrast, the land in the southeast, where the rainfall is much higher, is very fertile.

Above left: Much of the Australian interior, is hot, dry and inhospitable, as seen here in the north of Western Australia.

Above: The Great Dividing Range in northern New South Wales.
Below: Lush pastures are found in Victoria.

The people

Until 1788, Australia was inhabited solely by the Aboriginal people. They are thought to have reached Australia across a land bridge from Asia about 30,000 years ago. At the time of the first European settlers there were about 300,000 Aborigines throughout the continent. The early settlers slaughtered many and drove others into remote areas. The Tasmanian Aborigines, who may have been Australia's first inhabitants, were treated with particular cruelty. By 1876 they were extinct.

Today, about half of the Aborigines live in cities or towns. The remainder have stayed in the outback, but few still pursue their traditional tribal lifestyles. Aborigines now number about 155,000, or just over 1 per cent of the population.

The first European settlers were convicts, punished by banishment from Britain, who arrived in 1788. During the past 200 years, people from all over the world have made Australia their home.

Above: An Aboriginal family living in a mining town in the Northern Territory.

Below: The Australian population today includes people from many ethnic backgrounds.

Above: Len McDonald who breaks up cars for scrap.

Above: Yolande Brooks is a deputy town clerk.

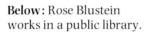

Below: Rose Blustein works in a public library.

Below: Ben Bevilacqua is a butcher.

Australia has become known as the "country of opportunity." About four million migrants from more than 120 countries have settled in Australia since World War II. Most have come from Britain, but there are also many from other European countries, particularly Italy, Greece, Yugoslavia and Turkey. In the 1980s an increasing number of immigrants have come from Asia, especially refugees from Indochina.

The image of the typical Australian, either as a hardy bushman or as a brash and noisy person, is changing. Although such types do exist, many of the "new" Australians have blended their different attitudes and cultures into Australian society. The majority of people also now live in cities.

Most Australians are outgoing, friendly and fond of the "great outdoors." They like to treat everyone as equals, and prefer a casual lifestyle with plenty of free time. Most Australians love to travel, both within their own country and abroad.

Above: Di Meier is a fashion consultant.

Below: Malcolm Thomson, a graphic designer.

Where people live

Australia is a nation of city dwellers; over 85 per cent of the population lives in cities or towns. Vast areas consist only of arid and scrubby desert and, compared with other highly industrialized, prosperous nations, Australia is only sparsely settled. Most of the population is concentrated in the fertile southeastern region, especially in the cities.

Four out of every ten people live in either Sydney or Melbourne, the two cities with the greatest concentration of industry. Since 1981, more people have been shifting away from country areas to the coastal cities. The capital city in each state is the main center of political, economic and cultural activities. Young people who have grown up in the country tend to move to the cities, either looking for work or to study at college or university.

Although the government has attempted to encourage people to live in regional cities like Albury-Wodonga on the New South Wales/Victoria border, people still prefer the main cities.

Above: The suburb of Paddington, with its attractive terraced houses, was built during Sydney's fast period of expansion in late Victorian times.

Right: Adelaide, capital and major port of South Australia, has undergone extensive development in recent years.

Country towns are friendly places with wide streets, low buildings and large parks and gardens, and have generally been well planned and laid out.

Canberra was created at the beginning of this century specifically to be the national capital and the seat of Federal Parliament. It was planned by Sir Walter Burley Griffin, and is set around an artificial lake. A high proportion of the people living in Canberra work for the government, although the Australian Capital Territory also includes some farming land.

Australians refer to the countryside around the towns as the *bush*. The interior of Australia is known as the *outback*.

In the outback some of the cattle stations are larger than the smaller European countries, and the homesteads may be several hours drive from the nearest town. A number of people living in remote areas of Australia do not have a telephone and communicate with the rest of the world by radio.

Above: Farms and ranches can be huge and very isolated.

Below: Townsville on the tropical north coast of Queensland.

Sydney

Sydney is Australia's oldest and largest city. It is also one of the world's most attractive cities. Sydney surrounds a beautiful harbor, Port Jackson, which is in fact the largest natural harbor in the world. Sydney Cove, now the headquarters of the busy ferry terminal at Circular Quay, was chosen as the site of the first European settlement in 1788 because it provided a safe anchorage and adequate supplies of fresh water. Today Sydney is Australia's commercial heart and the capital of New South Wales.

The Sydney waterfront is still a focus for both visitors and residents. Properties with water frontages or views are the most popular and command the highest prices. The ferries which criss-cross the harbor are used daily by thousands of commuters, and many other sorts of boats also regularly use the waterways.

Among Sydney's other natural and man-made attractions are the nearby surf beaches, the Opera House, Taronga Zoo and the Harbour Bridge which links North Sydney with the rest of the city.

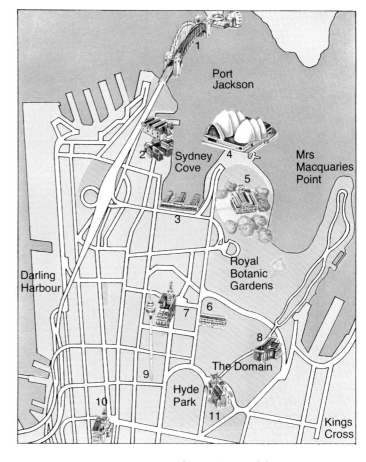

Above: Some of the main sights in Sydney:
1 Harbour Bridge
2 The Rocks Visitors Centre
3 Circular Quay
4 Opera House
5 Government House
6 Parliament House
7 Martin Place
8 Art Gallery
9 Sydney Tower
10 Town Hall
11 St Mary's Cathedral

Left: A complex network of roads carries traffic across the Sydney Harbour Bridge.

The main part of the city is bordered on the east by an almost unbroken chain of parks and gardens, comprising the Royal Botanic Gardens, the Domain and Hyde Park. The focal point of the city is Martin Place, a bright pedestrian plaza where many shoppers and city workers relax at lunchtimes while listening to street musicians.

Sydney's suburbs stretch to the north, south and west. Some are strung along surf beaches, some cling to the shoreline while others wind their way into the nearby Blue Mountains.

North Sydney has become increasingly important as a place of business, and high-rise office buildings dominate the skyline there. Despite moves to decentralize, Sydney, together with Newcastle to the north and Wollongong just south, still supports the largest concentration of manufacturing industries in Australia. Sydney is also a major port for national and international shipping.

Above: Looking south to Botany Bay, Sydney's main industrial port.

Below: Manly is one of Sydney's oldest beach suburbs.

Fact file: land and population

Key facts

Location: Australia is part of Oceania. It lies in the Southern Hemisphere, roughly between latitudes 10° and 44° South.

Main parts: Australia contains six states and two mainland territories. It also has several external territories: the uninhabited Ashmore and Cartier Islands, the Cocos (Keeling) Islands (pop 600) and Christmas Island (pop 3,000) in the Indian Ocean; the uninhabited Coral Sea Islands off northeastern Australia, and Norfolk Island (pop 2,000) also in the Pacific; other territories, both uninhabited, are Heard and McDonald Islands in the Antarctic Ocean and the Australian Antarctic Territory.

Area: 7,682,300 sq km (2,996,200 sq miles).

Population: 15,851,800 (1985 estimate).

Capital city: Canberra.

Major cities (1983 population):
Sydney (3,333,000)
Melbourne (2,865,000)
Brisbane (1,138,000)
Adelaide (969,000)
Perth (969,000)
Newcastle (414,000)
Canberra (256,000)
Wollongong (235,000)
Hobart (174,000)
Geelong (143,000)
Darwin (63,000)

Official language: English.

Highest point: Mount Kosciusko, 2,228 m (7,310 ft) above sea-level.

Lowest point: Lake Eyre, 12 m (38 ft) below sea-level.

Longest river: The Darling River, a tributary of the Murray River, is 2,700 km (1,703 miles) long, but much of its course is dry in winter. The Murray is the longest permanently flowing river. It rises in the Snowy Mountains and flows westwards for 2,590 km (1,609 miles), reaching the sea southeast of Adelaide.

Largest lake: Lake Eyre, 9,300 sq km (3,590 sq miles).

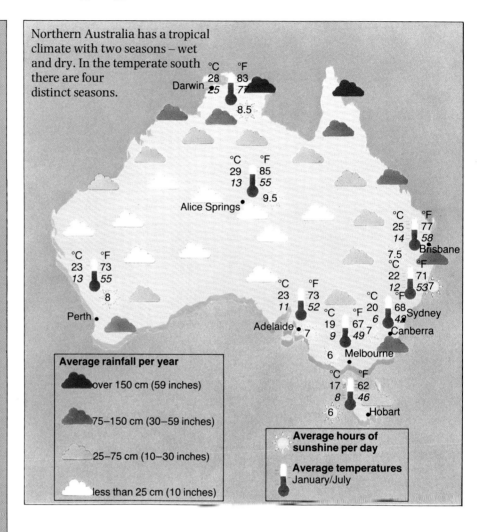

Northern Australia has a tropical climate with two seasons – wet and dry. In the temperate south there are four distinct seasons.

Darwin °C 28 °F 83 / 25 77
8.5

Alice Springs °C 29 °F 85 / 13 55
9.5

Perth °C 23 °F 73 / 13 55
8

Adelaide °C 23 °F 73 / 11 52
7

Melbourne °C 19 °F 67 / 9 49
6

Brisbane °C 25 °F 77 / 14 58
7.5

Sydney °C 22 °F 71 / 12 53
7

Canberra °C 20 °F 68 / 6 42
7

Hobart °C 17 °F 62 / 8 46
6

Average rainfall per year

over 150 cm (59 inches)

75–150 cm (30–59 inches)

25–75 cm (10–30 inches)

less than 25 cm (10 inches)

Average hours of sunshine per day

Average temperatures January/July

USA

Australia

France   UK

△ **A land area comparison**
Australia's land area of 7,682,300 sq km (2,996,200 sq miles) is large in comparison with many other countries. Britain has 229,979 sq km (88,759 sq miles), France 547,026 sq km (211,208 sq miles). Australia is smaller than the USA which has 9,370,000 sq km (3,600,000 sq miles). Australia's coast-line is 19,200 km (12,000 miles), and its greatest east–west distance is 3,983 km (2,475 miles).

Australia 2 per sq km

USA 25 per sq km

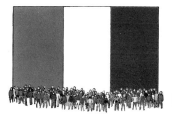

France 100 per sq km

UK 231 per sq km

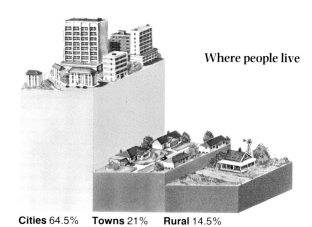

Where people live

Cities 64.5%   **Towns** 21%   **Rural** 14.5%

△ **A population density comparison**
Despite its very low population density Australia is one of the world's most urbanized countries. Vast areas are unsuitable for settlement.

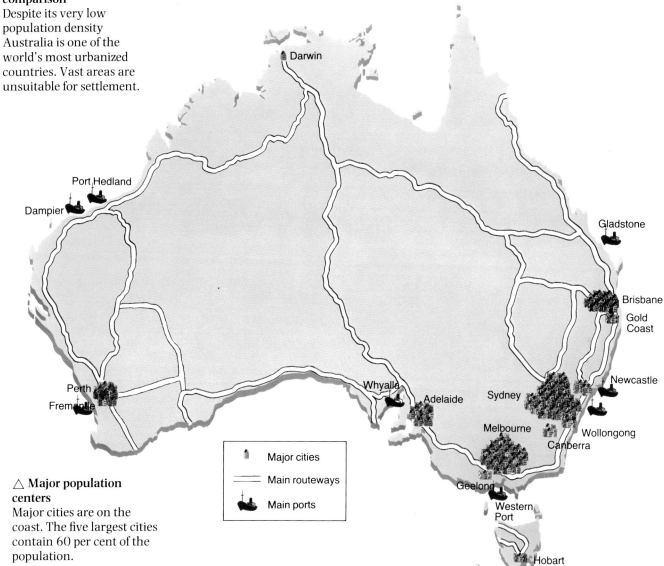

△ **Major population centers**
Major cities are on the coast. The five largest cities contain 60 per cent of the population.

Home life

Most Australians put a high value on a happy and stable family life. The average family has two to three children. There are, as in many other countries, an increasing number of single-parent families.

About seven out of ten households own or are buying their homes. The most popular type of home is a detached brick house with a tiled roof, surrounded by a neat, much-used garden. Nearly 90 per cent of families live in a house of this type. Most inner city areas also have many apartment buildings, both high and low rise.

Some homes, especially in the hotter parts of Australia, have a swimming pool in the garden. Large houses in country areas usually have wide verandahs to give protection from the hot, summer sun. Homes are comfortably furnished, usually with modern furniture. The sitting room is frequently the focus of much of the family's activity. Kitchens tend to be modern and well-equipped. There is usually a separate dining area.

Above: The Uilderks family live in a three-bedroom house in Melbourne. Grandmother has her own apartment.

Below: The family watch television together for an hour or so each evening after the boys have done their school work.

In many homes each child has his or her own bedroom, and most modern houses also have a family playroom. Back gardens often have a swing, sandpit or treehouse. Children are encouraged to make friends and bring them home to play.

Only about 10 per cent of elderly people live with their adult children and grandchildren. Often they live in a separate apartment behind the main house.

Six out of every ten mothers work to provide extra money for the family. Over the past ten years the number of mothers working outside the home has increased by 12 per cent.

Australians like to make the most of their leisure time, especially at weekends and during the long hot summer when there is more daylight. On summer evenings many families go to the beach, where they may swim or enjoy a picnic in the cool. Australians are, however, also extremely enthusiastic television watchers.

Above left: The children have regular chores. Justin helps his mother by drying the dishes each evening.

Above: The three boys share a bedroom.
Below: Travis feeds the family cat, Whiskers, after school.

Shops and shopping

Most Australian towns have a wide variety of shops, although the largest selection of goods is to be found in the capital cities. Country people usually travel to their local town to shop once a week. They will also visit a city once or twice a year on special shopping trips. Many goods are imported into Australia, and it is possible to buy anything from the latest French fashions to Japanese computers.

All suburbs have shops for everyday purchases. Most people also drive to a shopping center where there are one or two large department stores and many small specialty shops. It is usual for a family to go shopping together, often on Saturday morning or one evening during the week.

Many shoppers buy only their groceries at a supermarket, preferring to buy meat, fruit and vegetables from smaller shops, where they get more personal service.

Above: Most Australian families shop weekly in a supermarket. This is one of a large chain.

Below: Small local shops offer a wide range of products often bought direct from farmers.

Left: Large shopping malls are a fairly recent development. They seek to provide an attractive and trouble-free environment for the shopper.

Below: A typical week's shopping includes many packaged foods, both Australian and imported.

Milk bars or corner shops, selling a wide range of goods from newspapers to candy and groceries, are found in all areas. Some shopping centers now also have stores that sell Greek, Italian, Chinese or Vietnamese food. They are used by people of all ethnic backgrounds as Australians become more adventurous about what they eat.

Shopping can be a great challenge to people living in remote areas. Clothing can be bought through mail order catalogues, while packaged groceries can be bought in large quantities and stored. Ensuring a regular supply of fresh fruit and vegetables is more difficult, however. The water shortage also often prevents the creation of an adequate vegetable garden. The cost of transport can sometimes add up to 20 per cent to the price of goods in country towns and rural areas.

Open air markets, which tend to be open on weekends when most shops are shut, have become very popular. Products sold range from secondhand books and tools to many types of handicraft.

Cooking and eating

Australian people have always enjoyed a supply of good fresh food. Over the past 30 years the amount and types of food eaten by Australians has changed significantly. One of the main reasons is the influence of immigrants. The amount of meat consumed has dropped by 40 per cent since 1940, whereas more fruit, vegetables and cereals are now being eaten.

Most Australian houses have large, well-equipped kitchens. The majority of homes have refrigerators and appliances such as microwave ovens, food mixers and dishwashers are becoming increasingly popular.

Breakfast usually consists of cereal, toast, and tea or coffee. Sandwiches are the most popular form of lunch. The main meal of the day is eaten in the evening, when the family is together. The increasing number of working mothers has changed the eating habits of Australians. More packaged convenience foods are eaten.

Above: Australians enjoy a high standard of living and their homes have many time-saving devices.

Right: A family sit down to a chinese-style lunch. Wine is often drunk with meals. Children usually drink fresh fruit juice.

On average, one in every three Australians eats at least one evening meal out each week. Takeout food is also popular. Hamburgers, fried chicken or fish and chips are the most common choices.

A wide selection of restaurants reflects the variety of national backgrounds of the more recent immigrants.The most popular restaurants are Chinese, Vietnamese, Italian, French, Greek, Lebanese, Mexican, Indian and Spanish.

Hotels are also popular eating places, and most offer good, inexpensive meals. Many encourage the whole family to come, and often provide special servings for children. Some have play areas for children. Many hotels also have more expensive restaurants with more sophisticated surroundings.

Beer and wine are both popular drinks – almost all being produced in Australia. Beer is drunk ice-cold, even in winter. Low alcohol beer has been introduced recently and is gaining in popularity.

Above: Barbecues are a popular way of preparing a meal, especially in the hot summer months.

Below: McDonald's hamburgers are as popular with young people as they are in other countries.

Pastimes and sports

Australians have a reputation for being fit, healthy, suntanned people who like to spend as much time as possible out of doors. The many good beaches attract people who go there to surf, water ski, wind-surf and sail – or just to sunbathe.

On their vacations many Australians like to escape to the peace and quiet of the bush, or the coast. With a minimum of four weeks vacation a year, most families go away for at least part of this time. Camping vacations close to rivers, lakes or the beach are the first choice for many Australians.

Good facilities are available for many different sporting activities. Recent government-sponsored schemes have encouraged even more people to participate in sports to improve their health and fitness.

Many towns and cities have built bicycle paths to encourage cycling, and it is not uncommon to see entire families taking part. Many people enjoy jogging, and fun runs and marathons attract large numbers.

Below left: Mt. Buller in the Victorian Alps is a large busy ski resort near Melbourne.

Above: Surfing is popular on all ocean beaches.
Below: The Murray River provides excellent fishing.

Left: Cricket is a major spectator sport. The national teams of Australia and England are here playing a Test match at the Melbourne Cricket Ground.

Below: An Australian Rules football match. It is an exciting, fast moving game using both hands and feet, with 18 players each side.

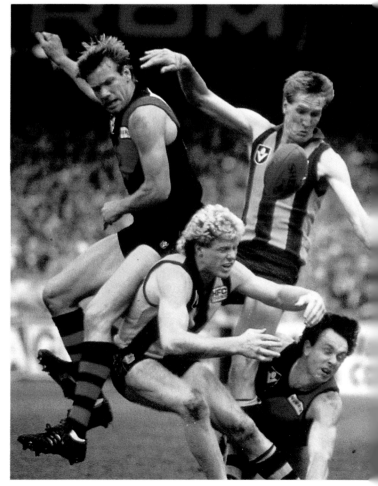

The most popular sports, played by people of all ages, include golf, cricket, Australian Rules football, athletics, rugby, soccer, swimming and tennis.

Australians also like to watch sports, although over the past few years less people have been attending sporting events such as football and horse racing because of increased television coverage. The highlights of the Australian sporting calender are the football grand finals and international cricket matches. Both these events always attract very large crowds.

Each main town or city has an art gallery, many with fine collections of both Australian and overseas works. Parents often take their children to galleries or museums on weekends. In some cities, as many people visit an art gallery on Saturdays as attend the main sporting events – a surprising fact for a traditionally sporting nation.

Big audiences also attend theaters showing the latest Australian, European and American movies, especially on Saturday nights, the traditional night out. Every city also has several theaters that show live dramas.

News and broadcasting

Australians have a newspaper readership which is among the highest in the world. More than 500 newspapers are published, including the major daily and Sunday papers. Because of Australia's mixture of cultures, some publications, as well as a number of radio and television programs, cater specifically for the different ethnic groups.

Australia also has a thriving magazine industry. *The Australian Women's Weekly* is the most popular; over one million copies of each issue are printed. Other popular periodicals cover such subjects as fashion, pop music, motoring and sports.

Almost every home has a television and a radio. Most cars have radios. Australians usually have a choice of three or four television stations except in some country areas. In some remote areas people receive television transmissions via the INTELSAT Pacific satellite.

Left: Some of the many Australian magazines. *The Bulletin* is a general news and information magazine.

Below: A wide range of comics and magazines are published for young readers.

Above: Most cities have two or three daily newspapers. *The Australian* is the only general newspaper distributed nationally.

Left: *TV Week* gives times and details on television programs and performers for the next week.

Below: A typical day's viewing on the various television channels.

Above: Paul Hogan has become a very popular television comedian through his witty observations on Australian life and people.

Below: Dame Edna Everage, played by Barry Humphries, is probably the best known Australian performer at home and abroad.

The ABC (Australian Broadcasting Corporation) has national radio and television networks. The ABC also operates Radio Australia, the overseas shortwave broadcasting service. The SBS (Special Broadcasting Service) operates multi-lingual radio and television services. It broadcasts programs from around the world, with English subtitles on foreign-language television programs.

The commercial television stations present a variety of programs, with many shows imported from Britain and America. The government stipulates the amount of Australian material they must show, however, and also the number and quality of the advertisements they are allowed to screen. Live broadcasts of sporting events from around the world, such as the soccer World Cup, are the most popular.

The introduction of video cassette recorders has proved very popular and changed the viewing habits of many Australians.

Fact file: home life and leisure

Key facts

Population composition: People under 15 years of age make up 27.3 per cent of the population; people between 15 and 64 make up 63.8 per cent; and people over 65 make up 8.9 per cent. Women make up 50.1 per cent of Australia's population.

Average life expectancy: 76 years in 1983, as compared with 68 in 1960. (By comparison, people in the USA live, on average, 75 years, while people in India live only 55 years.) Women have an average life expectancy of 79 years, six years longer than men.

Rate of population increase: In 1960–70, Australia's population increased by 2 per cent per year. The rate dropped to 1.3 per cent per year in 1973–82, and an average rate of 1.0 per cent per year is forecast for 1980–2000. A significant part of Australia's population growth is caused by immigration. The population has doubled since 1945.

Homes: 74 per cent of homes are owner-occupied, 20 per cent are privately rented, and 4 per cent are publicly owned

Work: Most people work a 40-hour week (or less), with equal pay for men and women in most occupations. The average weekly wage (excluding the highest paid) is A$374. The total workforce in 1984 was 7,127,500, of whom 637,000 (9 per cent) were unemployed.

Prices: Prices rose by 3.1 per cent per year in 1960–70, and by 11.4 per cent in 1970–82. In 1983–4 prices rose by 7.75 per cent.

Religions: In the 1981 census, 76 per cent of Australians declared themselves Christians, the two largest churches being the Church of England (3,810,000 members) and the Catholic Church (3,789,000 members). There are also 713,000 seventh Day Adventists, 638,000 Presbyterians, 491,000 Methodists and 421,000 members of the Orthodox Church.

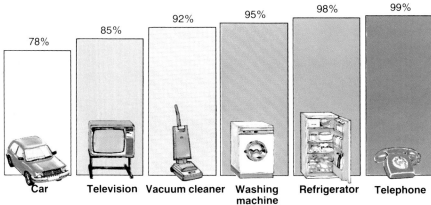

Car	78%
Television	85%
Vacuum cleaner	92%
Washing machine	95%
Refrigerator	98%
Telephone	99%

Transportation and communications	5%
Clothing and footwear	6%
Tobacco and alcohol	7%
Household goods	7%
Purchase of motor vehicles	14%
Food	16%
Housing	20%
Other goods and services	25%

△ **How many households owned goods in 1985**
Australian homes have a high concentration of consumer durables. In recent times microwave ovens and video cassette recorders have also become very popular.

◁ **How the average household budget was spent in 1985**
During the last twenty years Australian spending patterns have shown many changes. The proportion spent on food has fallen in relation to other items, especially other goods and services.

▽ **Australian currency and postage stamps**
Australia has a decimal system of currency – one dollar is divided into 100 cents. Coins currently in circulation are 1c, 2c, 5c, 10c, 20c, 50c, and $1.

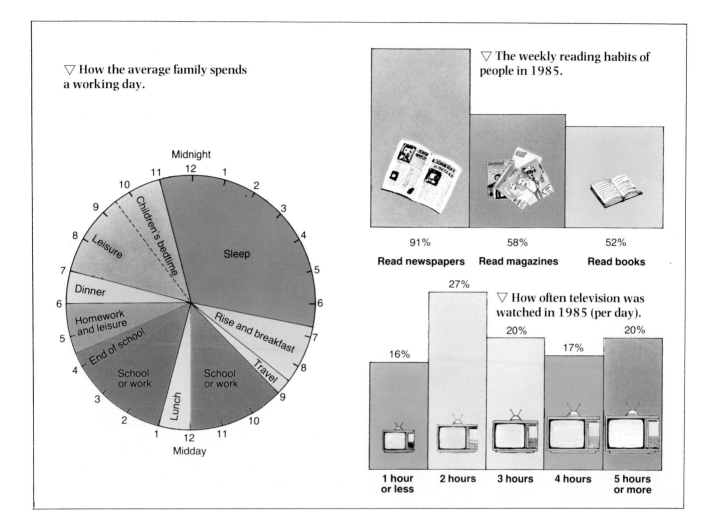

▽ How the average family spends a working day.

▽ The weekly reading habits of people in 1985.

91% **Read newspapers** 58% **Read magazines** 52% **Read books**

▽ How often television was watched in 1985 (per day).

16% **1 hour or less** 27% **2 hours** 20% **3 hours** 17% **4 hours** 20% **5 hours or more**

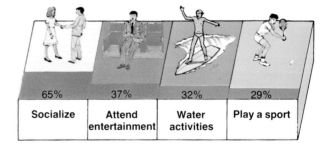

65% **Socialize** 37% **Attend entertainment** 32% **Water activities** 29% **Play a sport**

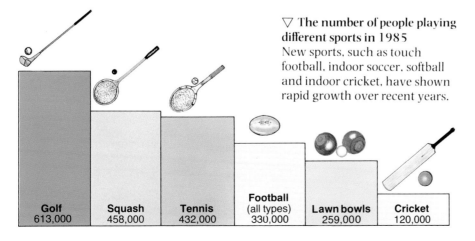

Golf 613,000 · Squash 458,000 · Tennis 432,000 · Football (all types) 330,000 · Lawn bowls 259,000 · Cricket 120,000

▽ The number of people playing different sports in 1985
New sports, such as touch football, indoor soccer, softball and indoor cricket, have shown rapid growth over recent years.

△ How people spent their leisure time in 1984
Twice as many men as women play sport. Social activities such as visiting friends are much more popular with women.

Farming and forestry

Australian prosperity was founded on its farming products and the country remains a major producer and exporter of agricultural products. Much of Australia's vast, hot interior is land that is suitable for rearing sheep and cattle. Crops of many kinds can be grown in the country's other varied climates, where the land is more fertile. Large areas, however, are too arid for farming.

Australia is the world's largest producer and exporter of wool. The sheep and wool industry is based on the merino sheep, which account for 71 per cent of the country's 139 million sheep. Australia produces a quarter of the world's wool. Huge quantities of beef are also exported each year.

The more fertile areas and coastal plains produce large amounts of cereals (the average annual yield of wheat is 13.5 million tons), dairy products, sugar and fruit. Tropical fruits grow in Queensland, grapes and citrus fruits in areas with Mediterranean climates and apples in Tasmania.

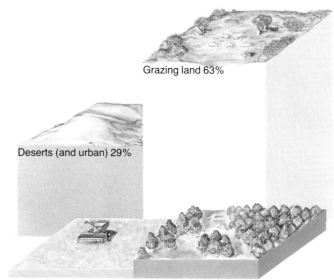

Grazing land 63%

Deserts (and urban) 29%

Arable land 2%   Forests 6%

Above: Land use in Australia. An inadequate water supply prevents farming and settlement in many areas of the country.

Below: Cattle and sheep graze together on the rich pastures of Victoria. The cattle here are being given extra feed before going to the market for sale.

Left: Queensland's hot climate and high rainfall are ideal for tropical crops. This sugar plantation is near Mackay.

Above: The Barossa Valley in South Australia has many vineyards.
Below: Eucalypts are the main timber trees.

Lack of water is a major problem facing farmers, and crop yields can be seriously affected by drought. Dams and other irrigation schemes have been built in many areas to give more control over water supplies. Most dairy farms are in the southeast of the mainland and in Tasmania, where rainfall is more plentiful.

Australian wines are now gaining a good reputation both at home and throughout the world. Almost 60 per cent of the country's wine is produced in South Australia.

The rich waters around Australia provide plentiful catches for the country's growing fishing industry. The most important commercial catches are tuna and salmon, shrimps and rock lobster.

There is some commercial forestry in Australia. Three-quarters of Australia's native forests are dominated by hardwood eucalypts, but commercial forestry plantations of softwood trees, mostly pine, have been established and are gradually producing more timber.

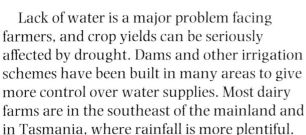

Natural resources

Australia is one of the world's major producers of minerals and ores, and has huge deposits of many of these commodities. Coal is the main source of energy in Australia but natural gas, oil and hydro-electric power also generate significant quantities of energy. Coal and gas contribute 87 per cent of the nation's energy needs.

Minerals account for over a quarter of all Australian exports. Most of the mining sites are in remote, hot areas, and attract people willing to work hard for a few years in return for high wages.

Australia is the world's largest exporter of iron ore. The mines in the Pilbara region of Western Australia, at Mount Tom Price and Mount Whaleback, are among the largest in the world. Australia is also the world's chief producer of bauxite.

Australia ranks seventh in order of world gold production and it is also a leading producer of copper, manganese, nickel, opals, silver, tin, tungsten and zinc.

Above: A miner in Coober Pedy, South Australia, shows off a piece of opal.

Right: Copper, silver and gold were first discovered at Mt. Isa in 1923. It remains a major mining center in northwestern Queensland.

Australia has about 18 per cent of the world's uranium, which is mined and exported for use in the production of nuclear energy. Various peace groups argue that the uranium ore should be left in the ground since it is also used to make nuclear weapons.

The main oilfields, off the coast of Victoria in Bass Strait, produce 75 per cent of the oil found in Australia. Smaller amounts are found at Moonie in Queensland and off Barrow Island in Western Australia. Despite these oilfields Australia still needs to import about a third of its crude oil refinements.

One of the most recently discovered natural resources is diamonds. Deposits rich enough to mine were discovered in the Kimberley region of Western Australia in 1972. The low quality of the diamonds makes them suitable only for industrial uses, but when in full production the mine will become the world's leading supplier of low-grade diamonds.

Above: One of the many drilling rigs in Bass Strait. Oil production in Australia only began in 1964.

Below: Hydroelectric power is becoming important. This station is in Tasmania.

Industry

Despite a comparatively small domestic market, Australia has a broad range of industries, many of which use advanced technology. Goods manufactured in Australia range from fashion garments to food, and from complex electronic devices and engineering products to plastics. There are about 80,000 manufacturing establishments in Australia. About a sixth of Australia's workers are employed in companies producing consumer goods.

Australia's bountiful supply of minerals has resulted in the establishment in all states of industrial plants designed to process the raw materials. Most smelters and refineries are located at ports, to allow for easier distribution of the finished products.

Australia has a significant motor industry employing more than 70,000 people. Five companies assemble cars, and all are subsidiaries of either Japanese or American companies. Some motor vehicle parts are exported.

Above: A foundry in Melbourne. Australia produces enough iron and steel to meet the needs of all its industries.

Below: A Falcon sedan being checked for quality on Ford's assembly line, where 450 cars are assembled each day.

The computer industry has grown quickly in Australia, as many organizations install and then update their equipment. About 12 companies assemble personal computers and many others produce software.

The country is one of the world's leading food producers. Much of the food is prepared for export. Food processing is the largest single section of Australian manufacturing industry. The main exports are canned fruit, dairy products, canned animal foods, beer and wine.

In addition to the large companies there are over half a million "small businesses" (each employing less than 100 people) which make up 90 per cent of all business enterprises. It is the ambition of many Australians to work for themselves.

Australia still imports many goods, particularly items such as factory machinery and construction equipment. However the country produces most of the consumer goods it needs.

Above left: Wing nuts being tapped and threaded.
Above: Checking microchips on a circuit board.

Below: Hamburger patties being made for a fast-food chain. They are also exported to several Asian countries.

Transportation

The provision of adequate communication and transportation services has always presented a major challenge to Australia. The vast distances and isolation of some areas means that rapid and reliable services are essential.

All the main cities, except Darwin and Hobart, are connected by rail links, and the railroads are an important means of taking goods to the ports for export. The longest stretch of straight railroad in the world runs for 475 km (295 miles) across the Nullarbor Plain in South Australia. Trains and buses provide the chief public transportation system in the main cities.

Private transportation in the form of the automobile has long been a vital part of life for most Australians – despite the inevitable traffic jams in cities. By 1988 it will be possible to drive all the way around Australia on a surfaced road known as Highway 1. It will cover a distance of 15,198 km (9,500 miles).

Above: Trains play an important role, particularly in the transportation of bulky goods.

Below: Trucks with two or more trailers are called road trains. Threeways is halfway between Alice Springs and Darwin.

Left: Air transportation plays a crucial role in the outback.

Below: Symbols of some Australian airlines. Qantas is the international airline of Australia. Ansett is an internal airline.

Qantas

Below: Electric trams remain an important form of transport in Melbourne.

Air transportation has been a major factor in helping to reduce the problems of travel within, and to and from, Australia. Today, however, the airlines are facing stiff competition from the interstate bus companies which offer a cheaper form of travel within Australia.

Small privately owned planes are also a major form of transportation in the outback. Most large ranches and farms have their own aircraft and airstrips. The Royal Flying Doctor Service provides medical care and evacuation facilities for people living in remote areas.

There are 70 ports of commercial importance. The busiest are Dampier, Port Hedland, Newcastle, Sydney, Gladstone and Fremantle. Others, such as Melbourne, Adelaide and Brisbane, serve the state capitals.

Ships provided Australia's connections with the rest of the world until aircraft replaced them as the quickest way to travel. However, most goods are still transported by sea, because this is cheaper.

Fact file: economy and trade

▽ **The distribution of economic activity in Australia**
Australia is trying to boost industrial development and thus lessen its traditional dependence on agricultural products.

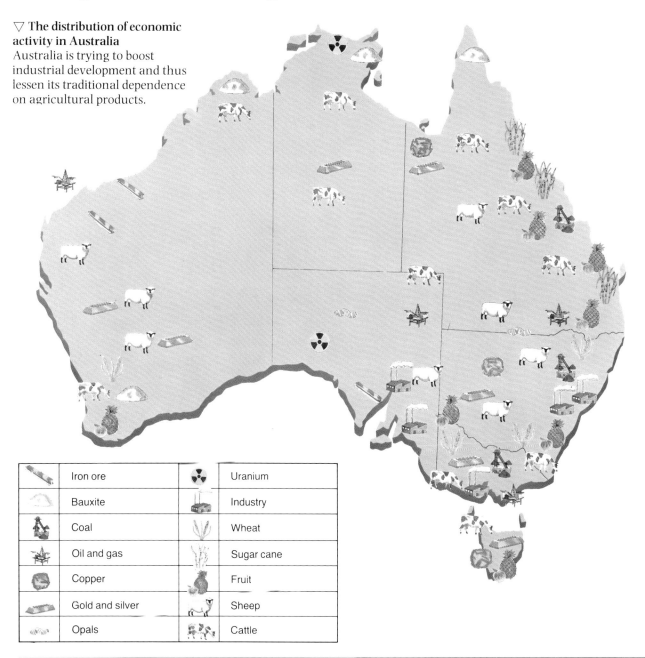

	Iron ore		☢	Uranium
	Bauxite			Industry
	Coal			Wheat
	Oil and gas			Sugar cane
	Copper			Fruit
	Gold and silver			Sheep
	Opals			Cattle

Key facts

Structure of production: Of the total GDP (the value of all economic activity in Australia), farming, forestry and fishing contribute 6 per cent, industry 35 per cent, and services 59 per cent.
Farming: *Main products:* wheat, barley, beef, fruit, lamb, corn, oats, wine, wool, vegetables. *Livestock:* cattle, 21,846,000; sheep, 138,625,000; pigs 2,478,000.

Mining: Australia is rich in minerals, especially coal, bauxite, copper, gold, iron ore, lead, manganese, nickel, silver, tin, tungsten, uranium and zinc.
Energy: Coal and gas contribute 87 per cent of the nation's energy requirements. Australia produces some oil, mainly off Victoria but also off Western Australia. Hydro-electric power stations contributed 13 per cent of Australia's total electrical energy in 1982–3.

Manufacturing: Australia makes most of the consumer goods (such as household goods and processed foods) and the iron and steel it needs. Australia imports producer goods, such as factory machinery.
Trade (1983): *Total imports:* US $21,806 million; *Exports:* US $22,062 million. Australia is the world's 18th largest trading nation.
Economic growth: Average annual growth rate of the gross national product (1973–82) was 2.3 per cent.

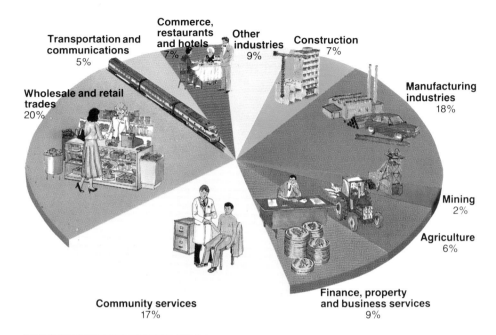

Transportation and communications 5%

Wholesale and retail trades 20%

Commerce, restaurants and hotels 7%

Other industries 9%

Construction 7%

Manufacturing industries 18%

Mining 2%

Agriculture 6%

Finance, property and business services 9%

Community services 17%

◁ **The distribution of Australia's labor force in 1984**
Two trends over the last ten years have been an increase in the number of part-time jobs, and an increase in the number of women working. The number of workers in service industries is growing steadily.

▷ **Australia's main trading partners in 1984**
Over the past 20 years Asian markets have become increasingly important to Australia at the expense of the traditional European ones. Japan has become Australia's biggest customer.

Australian exports

Australian imports (in thousand million US dollars)

ASEAN 2 1
Association of South-East Asian Nations

Japan 6 5

UK 1 1.5

EEC 2 3
European Economic Community (excl. UK)

New Zealand 1 1

USA 5 2.5

▽ **Australian imports and exports in 1984**
The bulk of Australia's exports are minerals and agricultural products. The agricultural share has dropped from 74% to about 36% over the last 20 years.

Imports

Fuels and lubricants 1.9
Transportation equipment and parts 3.2
Consumer goods 3.7
Capital goods (goods used to manufacture other goods) 5.1
Processed industrial supplies 5.4

Exports

Iron 1.5
Wheat and flour 1.7
Wool 1.8
Non-ferrous ores 1.9
Coal and coke 3.0

(in thousand million US dollars)

Education

Australian children must attend school between the ages of 6 and 15, but most start when they are five. Free education has been provided in government-run schools for over 100 years, but there are also church-run private schools.

In recent years some parents have grouped together to form schools for their children. In remote parts of Australia children living too far from a school either receive their lessons from the School of the Air, using the Royal Flying Doctor Service radio network, or attend boarding school.

In the year before they start school most Australian children attend a kindergarten for three or four half-day sessions each week. Depending on the state, children spend either six or seven years at a primary school. They are taught the basic skills of reading, writing and arithmetic, as well as social, health education and creative activities. The school day usually starts at 9 a.m. and finishes at 3:30 p.m., with one hour for lunch.

Above: Kindergartens today often have to cater for immigrants from many ethnic backgrounds.

Below: A school library. Schools are generally very well equipped.

Above: Students relax at lunchtime at a secondary school.
Left: Primary school classes are usually very informal.

Below: The campus of the University of Western Australia in Perth. The first Australian university was established in Sydney in 1850.

After primary school, children transfer to a secondary school for five years (if the state has a seven-year primary school course) or six years (if the state has a six-year primary course). Here they study a variety of subjects, including English and mathematics. These high schools have become less formal in recent years, with teachers emphasizing the students' social development as much as academic progress.

Most children study a foreign language at school. In the past French was the main language taught, but now a wide range of other European as well as Asian languages is taught. Some children attend special schools on Saturday mornings where they learn the language and culture of their parents, such as Greek, Italian or Ukrainian.

At the end of secondary school students take their Higher School Certificate examinations. Some students then qualify for places at one of Australia's 19 universities or 47 colleges of advanced education.

The arts

European influences have played a major role in shaping the modern Australian arts. The country's writers and artists have also been inspired by Australia's own remarkable landscape and Aboriginal culture, as well as by the hardships endured by the early settlers.

The Heidelberg School, renowned for its soft, beautiful landscape paintings, was founded near Melbourne in the 1880s. Tom Roberts (1856–1931) and Frederick McCubbin (1855–1917) were two of the school's founders and best-known painters. Today, a number of living artists have achieved international fame for their work. These include Sidney Nolan (1917–), known for his paintings of the outlaw Ned Kelly, Arthur Boyd (1920–) and Brett Whiteley (1939–).

Two of the best-known writers, whose work achieved great acclaim around the turn of the century, were Henry Lawson (1867–1922) and A. B. (Banjo) Paterson (1864–1941), who both wrote about the hardships – mixed with humor – of life in the bush. More recently, Patrick White (1912–) won the Nobel Prize for Literature in 1973.

Above: An Aborigine works on a painting. The colors are made from pigments found in the central Australian soils.

Right: *Glenrowan*, a painting by Sidney Nolan from the series depicting Australia's best known outlaw, Ned Kelly. He painted these works in the 1940s.

Above: The Sydney Opera House is a famous landmark and the home of the Australian Opera Company. There are also regular performances of ballet and music.

Right: The world-renowned opera singer Joan Sutherland in *Lucia Di Lammermoor*.
Below right: A scene from *Storm Boy*, a film for children.

The Australian Opera Company is based at the Sydney Opera House, but performs regularly in other cities, both at home and overseas. Nellie Melba (1861–1931) was one of the world's most celebrated opera singers, and Joan Sutherland (1926–) has continued the fine tradition. The Australian Ballet has also achieved international recognition for its fine performances. Notable Australian composers include Percy Grainger (1882–1961) who became known for his arrangements of folk music, and Malcolm Williamson (1931–).

Since 1970 the Australian film industry has become a major force within the arts. It has produced many important films which have been highly acclaimed worldwide. Among the most successful have been *Picnic at Hanging Rock*, *My Brilliant Career*, *Gallipoli*, *The Man from Snowy River* and *Breaker Morant*.

The making of modern Australia

Australia was first charted, in 1770, by Captain James Cook. The first settlers arrived in 1788 to establish a penal colony under the command of Captain Arthur Phillip. The First Fleet brought 760 convicts and 270 soldiers and sailors. They landed at Botany Bay and moved to Sydney Cove in Port Jackson, where there was fresh water, more shelter and better soil. A steady influx of settlers resulted in Sydney becoming a thriving settlement within a few decades.

By 1836 settlements had also been established in what are today the cities of Hobart, Brisbane, Perth, Melbourne and Adelaide. These settlements became the starting points for further exploration into the interior. With a rapid increase in the number of free settlers and emancipated convicts, settlements spread quickly in all areas. The discovery in 1851 of gold in New South Wales and Victoria attracted many thousands of fortune hunters.

Above: Eastern Australia was claimed for Britain on 26 January 1788.

Left: The early settlers had to endure long journeys to reach Australia.

Below: Wide streets and verandahs were typical of Australian country towns built during the 19th century.

Left: A meeting of representatives from the various colonies in 1890. **Above:** Canberra became the Capital City in 1927.

Below: Australian soldiers arrive in Britain in 1940. Australian soldiers played a significant role in both World Wars.

Self-government became an important issue as the various settlements expanded. The distances between them, and their isolation from Britain, caused great administrative problems. In 1850 the British Government passed the *Australian Colonies Government Act* which allowed the colonies to establish their own parliament and make their own laws. The Commonwealth of Australia, a federation of the six former colonies, came into being on January 1, 1901. The first Australian parliament opened four months later, with Sir Edmund Barton as Prime Minister.

Since gaining political independence, Australia has established itself as a politically and economically stable nation. Australian soldiers saw active service in both World Wars. In 1915 Australian soldiers fought at Gallipoli in Turkey and later were among the Allied forces in France. During World War II Australians were mainly involved in the fighting in Southeast Asia. Australian soldiers were involved in the Vietnam War.

Australia in the modern world

Australian society is undergoing many changes. Women are now taking a more prominent role in Australian life and have been appointed to senior positions in government and industry. The late 1960s saw the beginning of a sustained fight by the Aboriginal people for their rights. Since then, large areas of land in most states have been transferred to Aboriginal ownership.

In recent years, successive Liberal and Labor governments have tried very different methods to combat rising inflation, unemployment and industrial unrest. In 1986, after initial successes, the Labor government under the popular Bob Hawke was forced to make dramatic cuts in government spending.

Australians are becoming increasingly involved in issues that affect the quality of their life and environment. There have been protests against damage to natural resources, the destruction of rain forests and the pollution of beaches and rivers.

Above: An Aboriginal land rights march. The colors of the flag symbolize the yellow sun uniting the red land and the black people of Australia.

Below: Malcolm Fraser, Prime Minister from 1975–1983.
Below right: Bob Hawke became Prime Minister in 1983.

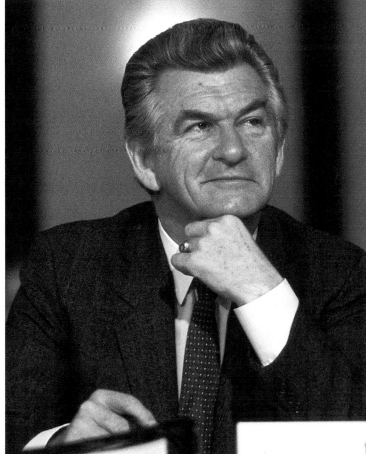

Left: The influence of the United States is clearly seen in this Sydney street. **Above:** Many high technology subjects are being developed.

Below: The winning of the America's Cup by Australia II in 1983 gave a further reason for pride in Australia and her achievements.

Australia has been an independent nation since 1901 but its political, social and economic ties with Britain remained firm until the 1960s. After Australia became involved in the Vietnam War stronger ties were made with the United States. Britain's entry into the European Economic community further weakened Australia's links with Britain. Australia however remains a member of the British Commonwealth of Nations. Today, American influences play a greater part in shaping many aspects of Australian life than do British. Australia has, however, established its own unique personality and traditions.

Australians are also vitally concerned about keeping peace both in the Pacific region and in the world as a whole. Today, the country recognizes the growing importance of its position as one of the largest and most influential countries in Southeast Asia, and is striving to strengthen the ties with its near neighbors.

Fact file: government and world role

Key facts

Official name: Commonwealth of Australia.

National flag: Based on the British Blue Ensign.

Anthems: "Advance Australia Fair" (national); "God Save the Queen" (royal).

National government: *Head of State*: The British monarch, represented by a Governor-General who is in turn appointed on the recommendation of the prime minister, the leader of the majority political party or coalition. *Federal parliament*: There is a 64-member Senate (10 members from each state and 2 each from the mainland territories), and a House of Representatives, which had 125 members in 1980.

State and local government: Each state has its own governor, who represents the British monarch, parliament and government. The Australian Capital Territory has an advisory House of Assembly. *State capitals*: Adelaide (South Australia), Brisbane (Queensland), Canberra (Australian Capital Territory), Darwin (Northern Territory), Hobart (Tasmania), Melbourne (Victoria), Perth (Western Australia), Sydney (NSW).

Armed forces: Military service is voluntary. *Army*: the Army's strength in mid-1984 was 32,212. *Air Force*: the Air Force had 22,677 personnel in 1984–5. *Navy*: in 1984 its strength was 16,692.

Economic alliances: Australia is a member of the South Pacific Bureau for Economic Co-operation, the South Pacific Commission, the Colombo Plan, and the Organization for Economic Co-operation and Development (OECD).

Political alliances: Australia is a member of the United Nations, and of the Commonwealth – a free association of 49 independent countries which were once part of the British Empire. It has a defence agreement with the United States; and a Five Power Defense Arrangement with Malaysia, New Zealand, Singapore and the UK.

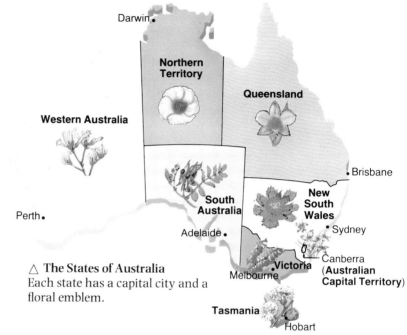

△ **The States of Australia**
Each state has a capital city and a floral emblem.

Legislative powers are divided between the Federal Parliament in Canberra and the six state parliaments. The Prime Minister has the most powerful political position. He is chosen by the party which has the majority of seats in Parliament and takes important decisions in consultation with his Cabinet. The Governor General, the representative of the British monarch, takes no part in the daily affairs of the government.

The Crown

Governor General

Prime Minister

GOVERNMENT

Cabinet

PARLIAMENT

House of Representatives (Lower House)

Senate (Upper House)

Electorate

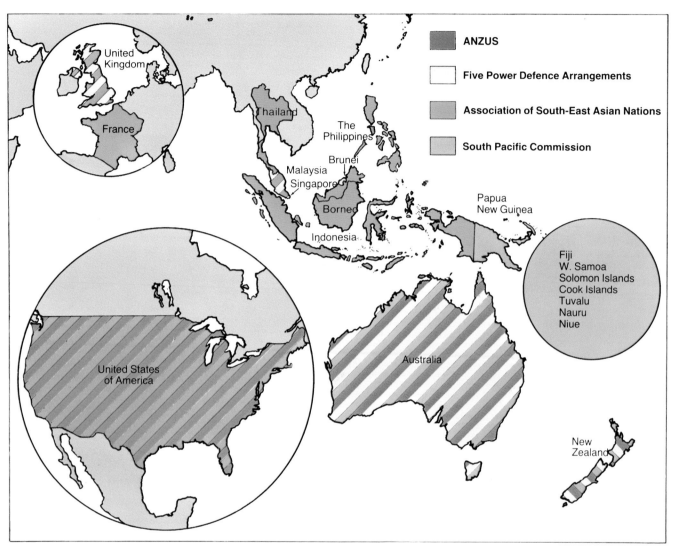

ANZUS

Five Power Defence Arrangements

Association of South-East Asian Nations

South Pacific Commission

United Kingdom

France

Thailand

The Philippines

Brunei

Malaysia

Singapore

Borneo

Indonesia

Papua New Guinea

United States of America

Fiji
W. Samoa
Solomon Islands
Cook Islands
Tuvalu
Nauru
Niue

Australia

New Zealand

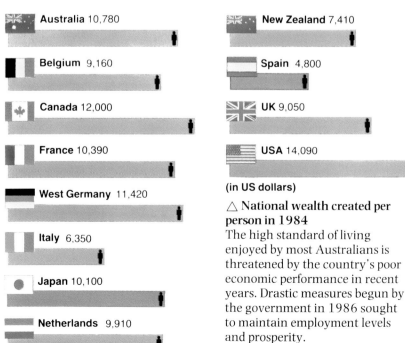

Australia 10,780

New Zealand 7,410

Belgium 9,160

Spain 4,800

Canada 12,000

UK 9,050

France 10,390

USA 14,090

West Germany 11,420

(in US dollars)

Italy 6,350

△ **National wealth created per person in 1984**
The high standard of living enjoyed by most Australians is threatened by the country's poor economic performance in recent years. Drastic measures begun by the government in 1986 sought to maintain employment levels and prosperity.

Japan 10,100

Netherlands 9,910

△ **Australia in the world**
Australia's most important treaties are with its closest neighbors, thus reflecting its position in Southeast Asia. Co-operation with New Zealand and the US through the ANZUS agreement is another basic feature of Australian defense policy. In 1986, however, New Zealand left ANZUS after disagreements with the US over the presence of nuclear weapons on the US ships in New Zealand waters.

Index